Munching Mor

The Characters

 Bear

 Lion

 Crocodile

 Dragon

 Cat

 Mouse

 Monster

Bear: I'm very hungry.
It must be time to munch.
I'll make a batch of
berry muffins for our lunch.

 Monster: Can I help you,
Bear?

 Bear: Yes, please, Monster.
You can put the muffins
on the table for me.

3

Lion: I'm very hungry.
It must be time to munch.
I'll make some juicy jumbo
burgers for our lunch.

 Monster: Can I help you,
Lion?

 Lion: Yes, please, Monster.
You can put the burgers
on a plate for me.

4

5

Crocodile: I'm very hungry.
It must be time to munch.
I'll make a crunchy crab salad
for our lunch.

 Monster: Can I help you,
Crocodile?

 Crocodile: Yes, please, Monster.
You can put the salad
on the table for me.

6

 **Dragon**: I'm very hungry. It must be time to munch. I'll make a dozen dunking donuts for our lunch.

 Monster: Can I help you, Dragon?

 Dragon: Yes, please, Monster. You can put the donuts on a dish for me.

Cat: I'm very hungry.
It must be time to munch.
I'll make a pot of sardine soup
for our lunch.

 Monster: Can I help you,
Cat?

 Cat: Yes, please, Monster.
You can put the soup
in a saucer for me.

Mouse: I'm very hungry. It must be time to munch. I'll make a chunky chocolate cheesecake for our lunch.

 Monster: Can I help you, Mouse?

 Mouse: Yes, please, Monster. You can put the cheesecake on a plate for me.

13

All (except Monster):
Our cooking is done.
It's time to munch.
But who has been
munching on our lunch?

15

All (except Monster):

Munching Monster!